THE GYPSIES

Bernice Kohn

THE GYPSIES

THE BOBBS-MERRILL COMPANY, INC.

INDIANAPOLIS NEW YORK

Permission to quote from *Les Tsiganes* by C. J. Popp Serboianu
was granted by Editions Payot, the French publisher of this work.
The passage herein is translated from the French by the author.
"Europe's Long-Harassed Gypsies, Ending Parley, Seek World
Recognition of 'Separate Way of Life' " by Bernard Weinraub

frontispiece drawing by Sarah Reader

THE BOBBS-MERRILL COMPANY, INC.
A SUBSIDIARY OF HOWARD W. SAMS & CO., INC.
PUBLISHERS INDIANAPOLIS KANSAS CITY NEW YORK

Design by Jack Jaget
Printed in the United States of America

Library of Congress catalog card number: 70-172348
0 9 8 7 6 5 4 3 2 1

In memory of David

Contents

THE GYPSIES

I

The Wragggle-Taggle Gypsies, O!

There were three gypsies acome to my door
And downstairs ran this lady, O!
One sang high and another sang low,
And the other sang bonny, bonny Biscay, O!

Then she pulled off her silk finish'd gown
And put on hose of leather, O!
The ragged, ragged rags about our door,
And she's gone with the wraggle-taggle gypsies, O!

It was late last night when my lord came home
Inquiring for his a-lady, O!
The servants said on every hand:
She's gone with the wraggle-taggle gypsies, O!

"O saddle to me my milk-white steed
And go and fetch me my pony, O!
That I may ride and seek my bride
Who is gone with the wraggle-taggle gypsies, O!"

O he rode high, and he rode low,
He rode through wood and copses, too,
Until he came to a wide open field
And there he espied his a-lady, O!

"What makes you leave your house and land?
What makes you leave your money, O!
What makes you leave your new-wedded lord
To follow the wraggle-taggle gypsies, O!"

"What care I for my house and my land?
What care I for my money, O?
What care I for my new-wedded lord,
I'm off with the wraggle-taggle gypsies, O!"

"Last night you slept on a goosefeather bed,
With the sheet turned down so bravely, O!
Tonight you'll sleep in a cold open field
Along with the wraggle-taggle gypsies, O!"

"What care I for a goosefeather bed
With the sheet turned down so bravely, O!
For tonight I shall sleep in a cold open field
Along with the wraggle-taggle gypsies, O!"

This old folk song has been sung for longer than anyone can remember. In the United States it spread from the southern mountain regions, where it has appeared in many different versions, but the original came to this country with the colonists from Europe.

The song expresses the "mystique" of the Gypsy—the lure of the exotic stranger. For in all times, in all lands, the Gypsy has been mysterious, exotic, in every way a stranger. Wandering from place to place, unburdened by material possessions, sleeping under the stars, speaking his own strange tongue, the Gypsy has refused to become assimilated. He jealously guards the secrets of his tribe, his language, his way of life. Few, if any, non-Gypsies have penetrated to the core of Romany mystery.

The lady who recklessly left her lord to sleep in a field with the Gypsies must have fulfilled the fantasy of many. Who has not been charmed by the footloose life of the wanderer? The Gypsies appear to have escaped most of the routine chores of settled living. The Gypsy child does not go to school. His mother has no house to clean; his father has no office or factory to go to, no fields to tend. Gypsies dance, sing, play, laugh, make love, cook over open fires, roam the face of the earth. They tell fortunes, entertain at fairs and carnivals, train animals and trade horses.

The perfect life? Not exactly. For the Gypsy mystery has generated two major reactions. The first, as we learned from the song, is attraction. The other is fear—and fear leads to persecution.

Gypsies have been reputed to be liars, swindlers, thieves, cheats. They have been thought by many to have the power to cast an evil spell by witchcraft or sorcery. The fear they have inspired has been partly responsible for centuries of discrimination in every part of the world. But it has also enabled the Gypsies to survive as a people and to keep their own identity. Their refusal to enter any society but their own—and their rejection *by* society in general—has enabled them to remain unique.

The scattering of the Gypsies to the ends of the earth has often been compared to the Jewish Diaspora. There is an important difference, however. While it is true that the Jews have their own identity as Jews, they have usually blended, to a greater or a lesser degree, into whatever land they adopted. They learn the language of the land, become permanent residents, follow the laws, do the same kind of work and follow the same social customs as their neighbors.

Gypsies do nothing of the sort. A Gypsy is a Gypsy no matter where he is, and he willingly follows no laws or customs except those of his tribe. He rarely intermarries and rarely enters any profession that has not been followed in like or similar form by his ancestors.

But instead of starting in the middle, let's go back in time and see if we can find out more about the history, the life and the romance of the Gypsy. We can't go back to the beginning, because no one knows where that is, but we can follow each path that leads toward it, and we'll come just as close as we possibly can.

2

The Wanderers

Long, long ago in far-off India, there lived a tribe of wanderers who roamed the banks of the Indus River in search of grazing ground for their water buffalo. Wherever a likely spot was found, the people raised their tents and stayed awhile. When the buffalo had eaten all the grass—or perhaps for other reasons that we cannot guess—the people folded their tents and moved on again.

But then one day the rhythm of the tribe's movements changed. No peaceful wandering now, no gentle meanderings along the stream, but *flight.* Flight from the familiar fields, flight from India, northward and westward into a world they had never known. There was no rest now, only movement, movement that in time would take these people many times across the surface of the earth.

What drove them from their home? Was it an enemy? Illness? Fire? Flood? The answer is lost in ancient times, in ancient places.

We go to the oldest records we have, but there are no answers there. We read, for example, in the ancient Arab history books about a wandering people called Zotts. For a long time the Zotts resisted the efforts of the Arabs to capture them. But in the early part of the eighth century a band of the nomads was finally conquered and driven into Kurdistan. A few years later a second tribe succumbed and was forced into Antioch.

Within a hundred years, in about the year 820, the Zotts had become so powerful that they were able to rise up against the Arabs and fight a bloody battle that lasted for fourteen years. Then the Arabs got the upper hand and captured 27,000 Zotts. The troublesome prisoners were immediately deported, some to a town near Bagdad in what is now Iraq, the rest to Ainzarba, a town that no longer exists but was probably somewhere in the Tigris River valley.

In the year 856 the *Roums,* or Byzantines, captured Ainzarba from the Arabs and thus became the rulers of the Zotts who roamed that area. The year 856 is usually given for the first appearance of Gypsies in Byzantium.

Why are we interested in this fragment of history? Were the Zotts Gypsies? Is there any connection between *Roum* and *Rom,* the Gypsy word for a Gypsy man? Perhaps. Perhaps not.

This is typical of all attempts to establish early historical accounts of the Gypsies. They were always called by different names in different countries, so that when we *do* occasionally find a story about a people who may have been Gypsies, we can never be certain they really were.

The Gypsies themselves have no written language, and hence no written history. Legends of family and tribe are handed down by word of mouth from mother to daughter. Whether or not they are accurate after centuries is of almost no importance, since no Gypsy would ever pass on such information to an outsider anyway. And so we go back to the history books.

There are records of wandering tribes that appeared in Greece in 1100. A monk wrote about a band of sorcerers and thieves who arrived at Mount Athos in that year. He called them *Atsincani.* By the fourteenth century, wandering tribes now presumed to be Gypsies had spread through the Balkan countries. And by the fifteenth century the history begins to be clear.

Le Journal d'un Bourgeois de Paris was an anonymously written account of Parisian life between 1405 and 1449. It contains the following passage:

> On Sunday, August 17, 1427, there arrived in Paris twelve penitent lords, a duke, a count and twelve knights. They were mounted on horseback and said that they were Christians and had come from Lower Egypt to make a pilgrimage to Rome to confess their sins to the Pope. The Holy Father heard their con-

fession and met with his council; he decreed that as a penance the Egyptians must roam the face of the earth for seven years without ever sleeping in a bed. However, he gave them letters stating that every bishop or abbot they met must give them a sum of money equaling ten livres.

When the men arrived in Paris, they had already been traveling for five years. The herd of commoners, one hundred and twenty men, women and children who followed the lords, were not permitted to enter Paris but were made to camp at La Chapelle Saint Denise.

Crowds of people came from all over to see the strangers. The travelers had pierced ears, and most of them, even the men, wore silver earrings. The men were very dark and had curly hair. The women were ugly and extremely swarthy. They had marks on their faces [tattoos?] and hair as black as a horse's tail. Their clothing was a length of cloth that hung from their shoulders by a cord. They were nearly naked, immodest and barefoot. They were the most wretched creatures ever seen in France. The women were witches who looked at people's hands and told the past and the future.

They stirred up trouble between husband and wife by saying "your wife [or your husband] has deceived you," and they emptied the purses of all into their own. This is what I was told but I visited them myself and I did not see them look at hands nor did I lose any money. Yet, news of the travelers reached the Archbishop of Paris and he said that he would excommunicate all fortune-tellers and all those who had shown their palms.

In September, one month after they had arrived, the strangers left for Pontoise.

This account of the Gypsies' arrival in Paris is quoted only because it is so precisely written and contains so much information. There were, however, other tales less complete but otherwise similar. By 1447, Gypsies had made their presence known in Germany, Switzerland, Italy and Spain. Always they claimed to be dukes, counts, etc.; always they showed their documents from the pope. Real or fraud? Another question without an answer.

Scholars working both backward and forward in time from 1427, the year of the Gypsy entry into Paris, have imagined the route they probably followed when they left India. Splitting into groups, some went through Afghanistan and Persia; others spread through Armenia, the Caucasus and Russia. Later they moved into the Middle East and Turkey. Some traveled along the shores of the Mediterranean and then into Egypt, along the north coast of Africa, and finally across the Strait of Gibraltar into Spain. The large numbers of Gypsies that remained in Turkey eventually fanned out across the Bosporus into Greece, and from there over the Balkan peninsula and into central Europe. In time they reached the British Isles and the Scandinavian countries. Much later they found their way to the new world, wandering throughout the United States as well as parts of South America.

How can historians even guess at the routes of migration if there were no written records? Chiefly through language. Romany, the Gypsy tongue, is the source of almost everything we know (or *think* we know) about the earliest history of these people. The reasoning behind this history is fascinating enough to deserve a chapter all to itself.

3

History Through Language

Romany, Romani and *Romanes* all mean the same thing: the Gypsy language. The name comes from *rom,* the Gypsy word for man or husband.

The *Romany chiv,* the Gypsy tongue, has many dialects, but basically all are part of one language. Many of the dialects are so distinctive that, more often than not, Gypsies from different areas of the world have trouble understanding each other, and sometimes cannot communicate at all.

Romany is Indo-European in character and is an outgrowth of the same northern Indian language that gave rise to Sanskrit. Sanskrit, of course, was the literary language of India, and Romany is quite the opposite—a purely spoken language belonging to a people who have no literature, or indeed no written language at all. While there are many theories about this lack, the most obvious is that a nomadic people cannot possibly establish schools or engage in formal education of any kind. Another very practical consideration, immediately clear to anyone who has moved with packing crates filled with books, is that books are heavy and bulky and certainly not suited to the Gypsy life. Books require a permanent home, not a foldable tent or a wagon.

But don't think that the inability to leave notes or write letters keeps Gypsies out of contact when they are separated from each other. They communicate extremely well through a sign language called *patteran* or *patrin.* (This seems like an appropriate place to mention that since there is no written Romany, all Romany words in this book, including the glossary, are spelled phonetically and are subject to many variations.) Gypsies almost never lose each other. A young girl who has *jumped the broomstick* (eloped) may come back to the campsite with her new husband to find that the family has moved on. The young couple will have no trouble joining them directly through patteran (literally, *leaf*), or trail language.

The first thing they will do is feel the ashes at the campfire site. The temperature will tell them whether or not the departure was very recent. The amount of rain that has washed over the ashes and the degree to which footprints and wagon ruts have been blurred or obliterated are other time clues.

At the crossroads, a few handfuls of grass appear to have been carelessly dropped on one of the four roads. The couple unhesitatingly turn up that road. At the next intersection there is a cross drawn with chalk or formed by two sticks. But it is not a perfect cross, since it has one arm longer than the other three. Again, it shows which road to take.

There are signals along the roadside, too, in case the patteran on the road itself becomes obliterated. A common signpost is a notched stick stuck in the ground, with another stick resting in the notch and pointing out the direction. A woven pattern of twigs in a low shrub would *never* be noticed by a *gorgio* (non-Gypsy) —and never missed by a Gypsy.

The patteran differs from clan to clan and may utilize anything at all that occurs in nature and that is easy to find. A few feathers stuck on a bush, some hairs from a horse's tail, a twig of one kind of tree fastened onto another kind of tree—all are patteran; also, a strip of bark or a rag, a stick with a strip of bark peeled from one side and left hanging, or removed entirely, and so on.

The patteran is used not only to make a trail but as a living newspaper, to pass on any news of interest to other members of the tribe who might be traveling the same way. In at least one area, a white feather left near the campsite means "You can steal chickens in this vicinity." A piece of tin on the ground means that the campsite is a good one. A lilac or an elder branch tells of illness in the tribe. A charred branch announces a death, while fir branches tell of a wedding. Willow branches mean a birth, and if they bear a bit of red thread, it's a boy; white thread, a girl. Warnings of trouble with the local police are shown with birch limbs or paper.

In cities or towns where Gypsies often do peddling or begging, they use a different kind of patteran that is similar to tramp or hobo language anywhere. This consists of chalked marks near the door of a house that tell the next comers what to expect. The mark may tell that the occupant is a superstitious person who will pay generously for fortune-telling. Other marks warn of a dangerous dog, a man with a gun, a policeman or local official, people who are hostile. While the signs differ, a circle is usually an encouraging sign, while a triangle means trouble. In England a stick with two strips of dangling bark is a danger signal, while a piece of rag tied in the hedge means that here is a good place to stop.

Gypsies who tell fortunes often help each other by passing on information that will make the next reading nothing short of astonishing. Two wavy lines tell that a childless woman is most eager to have a baby; wavy lines with a circle tell that the occupant of the house is either a widow or a widower.

But enough of the patteran trail, and back to spoken Romany. The present-day languages of India, including Hindi, Gujarati, Marathi and Cashmiri, have the same source as Romany. Perhaps Romany resembles Hindi a bit more than it does the others, chiefly because its sentence structure and much of its grammar are the same. Just a few examples will show the close relationship of Romany to Indian languages. Here are the cardinal numbers from 1 to 5 in Hindi and in five Romany dialects:

	Hindi	*Roumanian Romany*	*Greek Romany*	*Armenian Romany*	*Syrian Romany*
1.	ek	ék	yek	yaku	yoka
2.	do	dui	dui	dui	di
3.	tin	trin	trin	t'rin	taran
4.	car	chtar	(i) star	ch'tar	star
5.	pansh	pansh	pansh'	bensh'	punj

A comparison of some Hindustani words with Romany is also convincing: The Hindustani words for water and knife are *pani* and *churi*. The Gypsies of Persia say *pani* and *cheri*. In Norway the Romany words are *pani* and *tjuri;* in Siberia *panji* and *tschuri;* in Armenia, Egypt and England, *pani* and *churi;* and in Brazil, *panin* and *churin*.

Basic Romany as it is spoken today includes many words from Armenian, Greek, Persian, Roumanian, Bulgarian and Czech. The historians reason that if these languages have found their way into Romany, then the Gypsies must have migrated by way of the parent countries. And by the same reasoning, if a *large* number of words entered the Romany vocabulary, it proves that the Gypsies spent a long time exposed to that language, hence tarried a long time in that country. We cannot repeat too often that this is only a theory. It may or may not be true, but it's the best we have to go on. And so, since there are more Greek words than any other borrowed words in Romany, it is assumed that the Gypsies had a lengthy stay in Greece before they moved on. Or they mingled with Greeks in Asia Minor. There are also many Romany words derived from Iranian and Slavonic languages, indicating long sojourns in those countries, too.

If we leave the broad areas of Romany and study the dialects, we can learn even more about the migrations. The language of the Spanish Gypsies, *Caló,* contains many Arabic words but no German. We therefore form our theory that the *Gitanos,* the Spanish Gypsies, made their entrance into Spain through Africa and not through Europe. Similarly, the Romany Finnish dialect contains Swedish words but no Russian words. The wanderers must have approached Finland from the west.

While Romany has adopted words from the language of every country visited, most of those languages have been enriched by Romany as well. While there are innumerable examples of a Romany legacy in most European languages, only one comes to mind for English. It is our word *pal* from the Romany *pal, phal,* or *phral,* all deriving from the Sanskrit *bhrater,* brother. Of course we know that Gypsies were late in getting to England, even later crossing to the United States.

One of the numerous points of confusion in establishing the migration routes is the fact, mentioned before, that Gypsies have always been known by different names in different countries. Our English word Gypsy comes from Egyptian, since it was believed originally that these swarthy people had come from Egypt. The nomads were also widely known as Bohemians, Saracens, Luri, Lali, Luli, Karaki, Tsiganos, Gingari, and Bulgari, as well as by many other designations. A common name running throughout modern history is the Gypsies' own word *Romanichal,* son of Rom. In Spain Gypsies are known as Gitanos; in France, Gitans, Bohémiens or Tsiganes.

Where does this leave us with our history, then? Still confused, to be sure, but there *are* some generally accepted dates for the first appearance of the Gypsies in various places. They are:

BOHEMIA	*around* 1300
CORFU	1346
SERBIA	1348
SWITZERLAND	1414
GERMANY	1417
THROUGHOUT SOUTHEASTERN EUROPE	1417–1438
SPAIN	1447
SCOTLAND	*around* 1500
RUSSIA	1500
SWEDEN	1515

Today there is a very roughly estimated population of five million Gypsies throughout the world. They are found in almost every country and can be divided into three major groups, the Kalderash, the Gitanos and the Manush.

The Kalderash came principally from central Europe and the Balkans. They are still found there as well as in France, Turkey and the United States.

The Gitanos travel chiefly in Spain, Portugal, southern France and North Africa.

The Manush live mostly in France, Germany and Italy.

Once again, none of these "facts" is hard and fast. Gypsies generally do not make a point of registering with local authorities (even when required); they are not likely to take part in a census survey, and when they *do* get involved in some sort of record taking, they usually do not designate themselves as Gypsies. They are frequently recorded simply as foreigners.

Perhaps this chapter should have borne the warning: *Caution. The contents of this chapter to be taken at your own risk!*

4

The Gypsy Life

Now that we have some history behind us, we can move into relatively modern times and see what the Gypsies' life was like after they became established in Europe.

Contrary to our unknown French writer of the fifteenth century, Gypsies are a handsome people. Most typically, they are dark-haired and dark-eyed and have swarthy complexions. However, some strains of Gypsies have very light hair and eyes and are recognizable as Gypsies more by their colorful dress and abundant jewelry than by their physical characteristics. Gypsies are very animated and have a natural grace of movement. This grace undoubtedly accounts for, or is a result of, their outstanding skill as dancers.

The women traditionally wear long, colorful printed

skirts, sometimes several at a time, one on top of the other. This custom may have originated as a practical way to pack when on the move. Blouses are low-cut and brightly colored or embroidered. The women wear large quantities of jewels, often many strings of beads, gold chains, golden earrings and numerous rings and bracelets. Again, this is a practical matter for nomads. Since banks are useless to people who may never come back to the same place, the Gypsy family carries its wealth wherever it goes. What better way to do it than to adorn the women?

The men dress much more conventionally and are apt to wear an ordinary-looking pair of slacks with a sport shirt and a bright neckerchief knotted in front. In former times, Gypsy men dressed almost as colorfully as the women, being especially fond of velvet suits with silver buttons.

By now we have made it very clear that Gypsies are nomads. Although that means they move from place to place, it does *not* mean that there has never been any Gypsy anyplace who has settled down to become a permanent resident. Of course there are some sedentary Gypsies, sedentary by choice or by law—but in spite of laws, Gypsies have traveling "in their blood," and relatively few ever really settle anywhere even today.

More common than the really sedentary Gypsy is the semi-permanent one. He may settle in just for the cold months in a store front, a rooming house, or even an apartment or a house.

An examination of such living quarters must have shocked more than one innocent landlady or landlord. Gypsies don't carry beds; they like to bed down on the floor, all in one room. Copying caravan life even more, they much prefer to do the cooking on a small portable stove right in that same room rather than in a kitchen. There is no furniture and no excess baggage, for with the first breath of spring weather the entire family will be out the door and on the road again.

Some Gypsies travel more or less within the borders of a single country; many cover almost the entire globe and can certainly be classed among the world's most experienced travelers.

In addition to a shunning of material possessions, the nomadic life carries with it certain other modes of behavior. Few Gypsies are educated, because they have never stayed in one place long enough to go to school. They have never learned any form of farming or gardening but have become great animal trainers, breeders and dealers. Obviously animals can be taken on the road, whereas farms cannot. The Gypsy word for a non-Gypsy is *gorgio* (or *gajo*), which also means peasant, serf, clodhopper or country bumpkin. Since there is unmistakable contempt in the use of the term *gorgio*, we may assume that the Gypsy tends to look down on anyone who either tills the soil or stays put on it.

Another outgrowth of the nomadic life may be the Gypsies' reputation as thieves. Since Gypsies have never owned land or "things," they always help themselves to whatever they need. In more primitive times it was entirely natural for anyone traveling the countryside to help himself to firewood, fresh water, fruit or small wild animals. From there it was only the smallest step, as the land became more settled, to "borrow" milk from a cow, a chicken from the barnyard or wood from the woodpile. Needless to say, this free-and-easy attitude toward private possessions has never been very popular with the gorgios. The result has been open warfare. There is no country in the world where Gypsies do not have the reputation of being thieves who will "take anything that is not nailed down." They are also regarded as outrageous liars and swindlers in business dealings.

There is some truth in all of this, but possibly with good reason. The Gypsy has maintained his state of warfare with the gorgios. He would never treat them with honor and fairness as he would another Gypsy. Gorgios are not mingled with, never accepted socially—unless they are in a Gypsy's home, where the rules of hospitality are paramount. The Gypsy keeps his distance, his "separateness," by maintaining a wall of strict secrecy around himself. Part of the method is to tell a gorgio nothing that is true and to fool him whenever possible in any way possible. To sell a gorgio a lame horse and to be handsomely paid for telling the fortune of his gullible wife are great forms of Gypsy sport. The Gypsy takes pride and delight in his ability to fool gorgios and shrugs his shoulders when doors are locked or pocketbooks clutched at his approach.

The Gypsy's lack of a permanent address also makes him suspect—and again, often with good cause. If he steals or cheats a gorgio, the police may be notified—but then what? In all likelihood the name he has given is false. Even if it isn't, how do you find him? He won't be listed in the telephone directory. If you *do* know where he camps or lives, he can easily pack up his family and everything he owns and be gone in less than five minutes. After all, his home is on wheels.

The earliest Gypsies must have traveled on foot and then acquired donkeys or horses. After they arrived in Europe they began to use wagons drawn by these animals or oxen. By the early nineteenth century the romantic horse-dawn caravan, the *vardo, vurdon* or *verdine,* had become the trademark of the European Gypsy.

These brilliantly painted caravans can still be seen in many countries, especially in eastern Europe. In addition to red, yellow, green and blue paint, the vardos are usually handsomely decorated with elaborate carving. The carving is done with an ordinary knife. It is precise and very beautiful and may run all the way around the wagon and even along the shafts. Typical designs are geometric—diamonds, rectangles, triangles or squares.

The entrance to a vardo is at the front end between the shafts so that the driver can talk with his family during the journey. Just inside the entrance there is a stove with a stovepipe that extends through the roof. In Britain, where driving is done on the left side of the road, the stove is always on the right side of the wagon so that the stovepipe will be near the center of the road away from overhanging trees. On the continent the plan is reversed and the stove is always on the left.

The stove, incidentally, is used only in bad weather. When the weather is fine, all meals are cooked over an open campfire with pots hung over the fire from iron stakes with hooks on top. A kettle and a kettle iron are the most basic Gypsy equipment for setting up house-keeping.

Opposite the stove at the front of the wagon there may be a chest or a locker of some sort for storage. The rear of the wagon is for sleeping and contains piles of rugs, quilts and feather beds. Straps slung underneath the wagon hold tools, a bucket, odds and ends and perhaps a cage or two for chickens, birds or other animals.

The old-style wagon is an enchanting and unforgettable sight to the gorgio. Unfortunately, vardos are becoming more and more scarce, and like so many other lovely things from the pre-machine era, they will soon disappear, for the modern Gypsy, although still a nomad, is quite likely to be equipped with a modern trailer hitched behind an expensive car. Or he may have a motorized camping vehicle. Most of these are as spic and span as any home anywhere and are complete with curtains, television sets and all the other trappings of modern living.

Less affluent Gypsies live in tents, and many still make their homes in caves. Probably the largest group of cave-dwelling Gypsies are the Gitanos of Granada, Spain.

The candlelit whitewashed interiors are very picturesque, but in the romantic caves up in the hills facing the ancient Alhambra a very brisk tourist trade is carried on. The Gypsies are busy showing their caves, performing on the guitar, doing brilliant flamenco dancing, telling fortunes—all for rather high fees.

Fortune-telling, dancing and music-making are all traditional Gypsy occupations, and that is not surprising, since *all* Gypsy occupations are traditional. From earliest times Romanies have been metalworkers, especially blacksmiths, coppersmiths and pot-menders. The last has created great controversy over whether or not the Tinkers of Ireland are Gypsies. While they appear to be unrelated, they are nomads and they pursue a Gypsy trade. Opinion on this matter seems to be divided about half and half.

The various trades connected with animals have also been traditional for Gypsies. Some of the earliest Gypsy reports in existence mention the trained animals that the strangers traveled with. For many years they had a virtual monopoly on training performing bears for circuses and other road shows. Their skill with horses was legendary, and while these animals were in vogue for work and transportation, Gypsies were prime breeders, traders and dealers. Keeping up with the times, many of these horse experts have become used car dealers instead. One might argue that it is really the same profession brought up to date.

Traveling shows have always attracted Gypsies for reasons other than their use of animal acts. Gypsies themselves are fine entertainers, and the flamenco dancers of Spain are famous throughout the world. So are many Gypsy musicians, including the famous violinists of central Europe.

Much of the music that we enjoy today, particularly the so-called Hungarian works of Liszt and Brahms, is based on Gypsy themes and rhythms. Franz Liszt was such an admirer of Gypsy music that he wrote a book about it entitled *The Gypsy in Music*. In part he said:

> What fascinates the listener more than anything else in this music is its rhythmic freedom, wealth, variety, and flexibility, which are not to be found anywhere else to the same degree. These rhythms change constantly, are crossed and tangled up with one another and lend themselves to the finest subtleties of expression. From the wildest fury to a lulling sweetness and the tenderest plaintive melancholy. From a battle-cry to a dance. From a triumph to a funeral. Passing swiftly from the fairy-rings in moonlit meadows to bacchic orgies. They are all characteristic, full of fire, suppleness, impetuosity, and the surging of waves. Full of invention and whimsical fantasy.

While the performing arts are surely the most spectacular, other popular occupations for Gypsies have always been basket-making, artificial flower-making, peddling, junk-dealing, and in England the rather unique specialty of making and selling handmade wooden clothespins. With the advent of the clothes dryer, this occupation probably has a short life ahead of it.

But there is always fortune-telling, long ago and now the famous occupation of Gypsy women. There are many people who earnestly believe that Gypsies have special power to foretell the future by reading tea leaves, a crystal ball or the palm of the hand.

While the Gypsy fortune-teller herself can tell you very persuasively how gifted she is in the art of divination, it is believed that Gypsies never practice fortune-telling among themselves.

You have probably noticed that every one of the traditional Gypsy occupations is one that can be easily pursued on the road. Even the blacksmith or other metalworker carries with him a portable forge and torch. He can set up shop at a moment's notice. It might be mentioned in this connection that a very common Gypsy surname is *Petulengro,* the Romany word for blacksmith. The name is a common one for Gypsies in Britain and the United States, but it has been changed to Smith.

Whether training bears, fixing cars, telling fortunes or making horseshoes, at day's end the Gypsy family is just as hungry as yours. Let's take a look into a Gypsy "kitchen" and see what happens there.

5

Hotchi-Witchi and Other Delicacies

In days gone by, Gypsies lived solely on what they could find each day. They gathered all sorts of wild plants, mushrooms, greens, berries and roots. They were extremely skillful at constructing clever traps for small animals, so that rabbits, squirrels, birds and rodents made up the meat portion of the menu. They used wild garlic, onions and other herbs for seasoning.

Today's Gypsy is much more sophisticated. He may still do a bit of trapping, but he often has a chicken coop hung from under his trailer, and he will certainly stop in town to buy salt, tea, meat and other necessities.

The traditional Gypsy meal is still, however, anything that can be tossed into the big iron *sastra* pot hung over the fire. Food left to simmer in the pot is safe for hours with very little care, so it is often left bubbling away while the Gypsies are off gathering other food, peddling, or conducting whatever affairs they may be involved in at the time. It is not at all unusual to see a very young child stirring the pot or adding wood to the fire when necessary. By the time they are three or four years old, Gypsy children have learned not only to take care of themselves, but to perform many simple tasks for the rest of the family. It is always the children's job to collect the firewood for the camp.

Little boys also learn at a tender age to be accomplished fishermen. Since Gypsies often travel near rivers or streams, fresh fish is an important part of their diet. Gypsies have never been fond of boats, so they always fish from the shore, and they have developed several techniques to increase the catch. They are credited with being the first people to use artificial lures for catching trout and other fish. This method is now followed by people everywhere, but there is one form of fishing that is still probably exclusively Gypsy: catching fish by hand. The requirements seem to be endless patience, extraordinary dexterity and years of practice. When the Gypsy sees a fish at rest in a pool, he reaches for it so slowly that his hands do not appear to move at all. When his fingertips just touch the fish, he begins to stroke it ever so gently just under the gills. The fish appears not to notice. Then suddenly, with lightning speed, the Gypsy hooks his fingers under the gills and lifts the fish clear of the water.

Whether fish or meat, anything that is cooked in the big pot with whatever the nearby fields have to offer—carrots, beans, potatoes, all spiced with wild thyme and other herbs—the final product is sure to be delicious and hearty. Heartiness is important, because, while the Gypsies are on the road, daytime hours cannot be wasted in lengthy preparation of meals. Breakfast and dinner are the two big feasts of the day.

Not every meal comes out of the sastra pot, though. There are any number of other Gypsy dishes, and probably the most famous of them all is *hotchi-witchi*. This specialty is known by the above Romany name in England, as *nigli* on the continent—and hedgehog in the English language. In case you would like to cook some hotchi-witchi, here is a recipe for its preparation:

Hotchi-Witchi

First, kill the hotchi-witchi by striking it on the head with a stick. Then put it on the end of the stick and hold it over the fire until all of the spines are burned off. When it is cool enough to handle, clean it inside and out and stuff it with beechnuts or chestnuts and herbs. Now roll the hotchi-witchi carefully in clay, making certain there are no holes in the clay. Put it into the fire and cover it completely with ashes. The roasting time will depend on the size of the hotchi-witchi, the heat of the fire and the thickness of the clay, so it takes a highly experienced cook to prepare this dish properly. If all is done correctly, the clay gets as hard as a flower pot, and when it is broken open, all of the skin has baked into it and comes off with the pottery. Nothing is left but tender, juicy, delicious roast hotchi-witchi.

If you don't consider yourself a sufficiently experienced hotchi-witchi cook to try such a difficult recipe, there is a simpler one. Simply open, clean and skin the hotchi-witchi and stew it in the pot with vegetables, just as if it were a rabbit stew.

Rabbits, by the way, are a favorite Romany food, and a hutchful of bunnies often hangs from the bottom of the wagon right next to the chicken coop. Gypsies like to trap them in the wild, too. Rabbit fur, one of the few furs that Gypsies use, is valuable for lining winter garments.

Badgers are frequently trapped, too, and so are pheasants, blackbirds and sparrows. A meal of any one of these may be followed by nettle tea or dandelion coffee.

A Romany may be absolutely passionate about his dandelion coffee. He likes it hot and he likes plenty of it. It doesn't sound too hard to make. Dig the dandelion roots in the spring just after the plants have flowered. Wash them and spread them in the sun to dry. When they are thoroughly dry, cut them into small pieces and place them in a pan over the fire to roast. Pound the roasted roots with a rock or a hammer until they are reduced to small particles. Rub through a sieve. Store the finished product in tins to use throughout the year.

Gypsies do very little baking, since the baking of

delicate cakes or pastries is not at all suited to the nomadic life. But that doesn't mean they don't like sweets. A typical Gypsy dessert is the potato-sweet. Boil a potato until it is about half done, then use a stick to make a hole through its middle. Fill the hole with jam and plug the ends of the hole with the pieces of potato that came out of it. Put the potato into the fire and bake it until it is done.

Another dessert is called *buni-manricli.* Boil some oatmeal, wheat or other cereal grain for just a few minutes. Drain it and spread it out to dry. Then mix it with honey, pounded nuts and butter, form the mixture into cakes and roast them over the fire.

Snails are a great delicacy when sprinkled with garlic, parboiled in salt water, rubbed with plenty of fat and roasted.

Eel, either fried or in a soup, is particularly good served with buttercup root. Cook the root along with the fish or serve it raw as a spice or in a salad.

Since Gypsies only rarely bake bread, they use other starchy foods as their "staff of life." One of the most common of these is cornmeal boiled in water. Cornmeal mush is, of course, not an exclusively Gypsy dish. It is very popular with gorgios as well as Romanies throughout southeastern Europe. In Roumania the mush is called *mamaliga,* in Italy *polenta.* Sometimes Gypsies make little cakes of cornmeal mush flavored with cumin and coriander and called *ankrusté.*

One of the reasons Gypsy foods are so tasty is that

they contain a variety of wild herbs. Gypsies are among the best herbalists in the world. Not only do they recognize every herb, weed, leaf or root and know its best use in cooking; they are also skilled in making herbal medicines for every sort of illness. Some of these "prescriptions," used by generations of Romanies, are almost identical with some of our most sophisticated pharmaceuticals. Many nomadic Gypsies today still much prefer their own remedies to those prescribed by a doctor. Their philosophy seems to be that if nature made the illness, nature can also cure it.

Among some Gypsy remedies are water in which willow bark has been boiled, taken to cure rheumatic fever; chestnut leaves for bronchitis; periwinkle for diabetes; rosemary for dandruff or falling hair; root of lily-of-the-valley for heart trouble.

Animal parts are used for medicines, too. Pulverized frogs' livers and tongues mixed with crushed beetles and brandy is a remedy for fever. Crushed beetles alone are used as a cure for many ailments, as is a concoction of pitch and fried onions!

6

Religion and Its Rites

If Gypsies have a formal religion of their own, they have kept it, like so many other things, a well-guarded secret. To all appearances, they adopt the religion of whatever place they are in, and then they are often extremely devout. They are Mohammedans, Catholics, Protestants. Whether they actually believe in the precepts of these churches, or whether the observance of religious rites simply provides an outlet for their innate belief in God and the need to express it, is hard to say.

C. J. Popp Serboianu, a Roumanian Gypsiologist, made this comment on Gypsy religious beliefs:

> They [Gypsies] recognize only two principles: The *O'Del*, God the Creator, the principle of good, and

O'Bengh, the devil, or the principle of evil, each of them, as it would seem, equally powerful and always engaged in struggle, one against the other.

All that is good and to their advantage comes from God; all that is bad and harmful to them comes from the devil. These principles are not abstract, but, on the contrary, become real in the elements of nature, which makes a sort of universal church. They have no ritual, no symbols, no prayers, but in their souls they have a religion which does not offer them a vision of a future life (in which, moreover, they do not believe: not any more than in the resurrection, in Heaven or in Hell), nor of Hellfire; it does not demand any payment from them for the salvation of their souls.

Be all that as it may, Gypsies are often enthusiastic churchgoers and like to take part in religious festivals and gatherings. Perhaps it should be pointed out that they also flock in great numbers to racecourses, fairs, carnivals and large gatherings of any kind.

The largest assembly of Gypsies today is the one that takes place in May of every year at Saintes-Maries-de-la-Mer in southern France. Romanies from all parts of Europe journey to this festival, which honors three Marys: Mary Salome, Mary Jacobe, and Mary Magdalene. In a recent year it was estimated that 8,000 Gypsies attended the two-day event.

The festival is a Roman Catholic one, commemorating

the landing, in 42 A.D., of the three Marys at this village. According to legend, they had drifted in a small boat, without oars or sail, from the Holy Land. With them in the boat was their Egyptian servant girl, Sara.

As Sara la Kali—Sara of the Gypsies, or the Black Sara—she has become the patron saint of the Gypsies. Before her statue at Saintes-Maries-de-la-Mer the Romanies keep an all-night candlelight vigil. Many of the women hang garments or bits of cloth on the image of the Black Virgin. The following day, they immerse themselves in the sea.

How these customs originated and why Romanies honor the Black Sara are more Gypsy mysteries. There are some scholars who believe that Sara la Kali is not even the same one that the Catholic Church acknowledges, but a different person altogether. This theory holds that the Sara who served the three Marys was a white Sara, while Sara la Kali (a swarthy Gypsy?) was onshore to greet the four voyagers when they landed.

The Sara ceremony and other Gypsy religious ceremonies surrounding birth, marriage and death are closely interwoven with old legends, shreds of ancient pagan religions and superstition. It is hard to say which is which.

We learn, for example, that the birth of a child must never take place within the tent or caravan. The mother-to-be retreats to an outdoor spot to bear her child. She may or may not be attended by a midwife.

As soon as the baby is born, the mother takes it to

a tent that stands apart from the rest of the camp. Here she is visited by other females, but she is considered unclean to males, and no male may even approach her tent. This includes the husband, who stays away from his wife for several weeks and does not touch his baby for a period varying from a number of weeks to almost a year, depending on individual tribal custom.

The midwife is considered permanently unclean. She is shunned by all men at all times.

Taboos relating to women, incidentally, are not confined to the period following a birth. At no time will a Gypsy eat food that has been touched by the skirt of a woman. Should the hem of a skirt accidentally touch food, that food must be thrown away.

While some Gypsies follow formal Christian practice in matters of baptism, weddings or funerals, many do not, but follow their own customs instead. And some do both.

The baptism of a Gypsy child calls for immersion in a running stream and the giving of three baptismal names. One is the public name that will be used for official documents (if any) and told to gorgios. Another name is a Gypsy name and will be used only by other Gypsies. The third name is the secret name. The mother whispers it so that no one can hear and then it is never repeated—although some authorities have claimed that the mother once more whispers the name to the child when he reaches puberty. The name is kept secret in order to fool the evil spirits. How can they find a person to harm him if they cannot find out who he really is?

Weddings, like baptisms, may or may not take place in a church or before a civil authority. Gypsy wedding ceremonies have many forms.

The simplest is called jumping the broomstick. The engaged couple sneaks out of camp one night and slips off to travel alone together for a while. If they don't have a wagon or other vehicle, they walk until they are tired, then pitch a tent and set up housekeeping. After a few weeks they return to the wife's family, and they are considered by all to be married. They may continue to stay with the bride's family from that time on, or they may travel for part of the year with that group and spend some time by themselves. This custom of women remaining attached to their families accounts for the very large size of some groups.

A more formal marriage ceremony begins with a formal betrothal. The young man offers the girl a gift, usually a head scarf or a handkerchief. If she accepts it, the couple are engaged.

Since chastity is of extreme importance to Gypsies, the betrothed girl is often examined by the old woman of the tribe who makes sure the girl is a virgin. If she is not, the engagement is cancelled. But if the old woman is satisfied that the girl is pure, she gives the signal and a white flag is hoisted for all to see. At the same time, a white dove is released and a special song, the *arbola,* is sung by the assembled group.

Among some tribes, the bride must now be purchased. The bargaining, often voluble, is carried on enthusiastically by the two fathers until a deal has been struck. When these arrangements have been completed, the word goes out and the tribe assembles. Gypsies will travel long distances to attend weddings, so they are often enormous festive occasions.

The ceremony itself is very simple. Sometimes the couple simply join hands and promise to be true to each other, then each feeds the other a bit of bread and salt. A bountiful feast follows and the merrymaking lasts for several days.

Konrad Bercovici, in *The Story of the Gypsies,* describes a wedding that takes place before a campfire within a circle of tents and wagons. The women sit on one side of the circle, the men on the other. The bridal couple are perched on a heap of rugs and skins. After the usual last-minute haggling, the father of the groom pays the bride price to the bride's mother. Then the oldest member of the tribe turns to the groom and asks him to swear to leave the woman he wants to make the mother of his children as soon as he discovers that he no longer loves her. The bride takes a similar oath.

How different such a promise is from *our* usual vow of eternal love! Following the oath, there is a blood-mingling ceremony. A small cut is made on the groom's left wrist and one on the bride's right wrist. The wrists are then tied together for a few minutes so that the bloods mingle.

As simple as Gypsy weddings are, the marriages are among the most stable in the world. While divorce is possible, as suggested above, it is rarely resorted to. Infidelity among married couples is almost unheard of, and there seems to be very little strife of any serious sort. The Gypsy sense of solidarity is particularly strong in marriage.

It happens now and then that a Gypsy marries a gorgio. The gorgio is never completely admitted as a member of the tribe. There is no way he can "convert." Even if he is accepted socially to some extent, the couple will never have full status within the group, and the newcomer will never be made party to certain secret matters. Mixed-marriage couples usually leave the tribe and travel by themselves. Their half-breed children are regarded with a certain amount of contempt by full Gypsies.

Funerals, like the other ceremonies, may take place with or without benefit of clergy. But one thing is certain: no one dies in his wagon, tent or caravan. A dying person is carried outside to die in the open air. If the weather is very bad, a tent (which will later be destroyed) may be placed over him. The tribe gathers around and waits. When death occurs, the wailing and mourning begin. Gypsies are very emotional, and their lamentations can be heard for long distances.

Since members of the tribe come from all over, there is usually a waiting period of several days before the burial. During this time, three men sit with the body while the other Gypsies sit around the fire. No one may take any food except bread and water and no one goes to bed.

When the body is finally placed in its coffin, a few favored objects may be put in also. If the deceased was a violinist or a guitarist, his instrument is usually buried with him.

The trip to the burial ground is made on foot, and Gypsies are very careful not to stumble on the way. There is a superstition that anyone who stumbles en route to a burial will be in his own grave within a year.

When the coffin is lowered into the ground, earth, water, coins—and in England, beer—are sprinkled on top of it. There is no wailing now, for this would disturb the deceased.

Some Gypsies drill seven holes in the coffin lid. The first hole, placed just above the forehead, is to make it possible for the soul to leave. Two holes for the eyes to see, two for the ears to hear (especially to hear the funeral music), and two below the heart in order that the essence of the body may pass through.

Now, heartbreakingly sad, weeping violins express the pain of the tribe. A quiet clapping keeps the rhythm. A slow dance begins, growing faster and faster as the dead person's spirit is lured from the body and through the holes in the coffin. Suddenly, all is silent and the coffin is covered with earth.

7

Magic, Witchcraft and the Evil Eye

From his first appearance in Europe, the Gypsy—that dark and mysterious stranger—was believed to have supernatural powers. Perhaps his exotic dress, his strange language, his outstanding gift for handling horses and other animals—in fact, his entire oneness with nature—seemed quite magical to the more conventional Europeans. Or the Gypsies may have convinced the gorgios that they could perform feats of magic. Or perhaps they themselves really believed they could. In any case, as long as it was held that Gypsies were magicians or sorcerers, they had a certain amount of power and protection. They also had a good source of income, since Gypsy women were—and still are—much sought after as fortune-tellers. There were other moneymaking opportunities, too.

One of the first great Gypsiologists to write in English was George Borrow. In 1841 he said in *The Zincali:*

> Dabbling in sorcery is in some degree the province of the female Gypsy. She affects to tell the future, and to prepare philters by means of which love can be awakened in any individual towards any particular object; and such is the credulity of the human race, even in the most enlightened countries, that the profits arising from these practices are great.

Borrow went on to say that the accusation that Gypsies cause disease and death among cattle was by no means groundless. He told of two methods that were used. In the first, Gypsies threw poisoned powders into the mangers of horses and cows. When the animals became ill, the Gypsies appeared and offered their services—for a fee, of course—as animal doctors.

Another more drastic trick was practiced chiefly on pigs. In this case, the Gypsies used a poison that did not simply make the animals slightly ill but killed them almost immediately. The Gypsies then asked the farmers if they might have the dead animals. The farmers were usually glad to get rid of the carcasses, and the Gypsies then had a feast, since they knew that the poison they used had gone straight to the animals' brains and did not affect the quality of their meat in any way.

Borrow is making the point, of course, that Gypsy

"magic" for killing livestock is pure Gypsy skulduggery. There is no question, however, that there is still a widespread belief in many rural areas of the world that Gypsies have the power to kill humans or animals by "black magic." One of the best known techniques of black magic is to make a wax doll containing some hairs or nail clippings of the intended victim. The dolls are then stuck with pins or nails or melted in a fire. The victim is supposed to die.

Another method is to pour water over a weeping willow branch for nine days and then pour some of that same water in front of the victim's house. The idea here is that the "weeping" will be transferred from the willow to the person.

The most famous Gypsy magic of all is the power of the evil eye. One who has the evil eye is supposedly able to bewitch or cast a spell over the victim just by staring at him.

Gypsies themselves believe in the evil eye and take careful precautions against it. A child is often protected by pouring his bath water over him, having first let the water run along the blade of a large knife. Children can also be protected by tying a red ribbon around their wrists.

Quoting from Borrow's *The Zincali* once more:

> In the Gitáno [Gypsy] language, casting the evil eye is called *Querelar nasula,* which simply means making sick, and which, according to the common

superstition, is accomplished by casting an evil look at people, especially children, who, from the tenderness of their constitution, are supposed to be more easily blighted than those of a more mature age. After receiving the evil glance, they fall sick, and die in a few hours.

So far we have discussed only black magic, but there is another kind of Gypsy magic, too. The herb remedies of the Gypsy women were a form of "white magic" used to combat the evil spells of others or to win the heart of a loved one. Many Gypsies, as we have already learned, are skilled in the use of herbal medicines and cures (as are most nomadic people who live in close communion with nature), and it is perhaps partly on this basis that their reputation as magicians exists.

While acts of magic are presumed to be possible for many Gypsies, the Gypsy witch is believed to be especially powerful in making trouble by means of her black magic. The witch is usually the daughter of a witch and has been trained from childhood in her hereditary art.

But witches can be created in later life, too. The belief is that a demon sometimes enters the bed of a sleeping girl in order to have sexual relations with her. The girl does not awaken and so is not aware of what is happening. However, in the morning she suddenly realizes that she can see into the past and the future. She then must find an old witch to teach her all of the arts of witchcraft, the casting of spells and the ways to combat the spells of other witches. When she has perfected her art, she is considered a true witch and is feared and respected as such by other Gypsies.

Even where no witchcraft is involved, Gypsies are highly superstitious and pay careful attention to omens, signs and "dangerous" practices. Here are some Gypsy beliefs:

A croaking raven foretells a death.

The wagtail (a bird) foretells that a friend will soon visit the camp.

If you find a broken flower on the road and pick it up, you will soon hear that a relative is sick.

If you see a moth flying in a house, do not kill it, for it is the soul of a dead gorgio that has come back to look for something.

A toad walking along the road means that an enemy is approaching.

A croaking frog brings news of a birth.

If a girl finds a bird's egg in the road, she will have a child within the year.

A black ear of rye in a field means that the finder will soon receive a gift of gold.

If you see a black man, a gray horse or a man with a wooden leg first thing in the morning, you will have good luck.

A woman with a wooden leg brings a curse.

A cross-eyed man means good luck, a cross-eyed woman bad luck.

Troubles are sure to come in threes. This is because

of the *trin bengs:* the devil, his wife and his son. When the devil bothers you, his wife and son must also have a turn.

If you kill a furbearing animal except for food, its *mullah,* or ghost, will haunt you.

If a bear dies (a superstition prevalent among bear-leading Gypsies) you must never skin him but bury him in his fur. If you remove his coat, the devil wears it and puts a curse on the owner. Here is:

A Remedy for the Evil Eye

Fill a jar with water from a stream, making sure that the water is taken *with* rather than against the current. Place in the water seven cloves of garlic and put the jar in the fire. When the water begins to boil, stir it with a three-forked twig and say:

Miseç' yakhá tut dikhen,
Te yon káthe mudáren!
Te átunci eftá coká
Te çaven miseçe yakhá;
Miseç' yakhá tut dikhen,
Te yon káthe mudáren!
But práhestár e yakhá
Atunci kores th'ávená;
Miseç' yakhá tut dikhen,
Te yon káthe mudáren!
Pçábuvená pçábuvená
Andre develeskero yakhá!

Evil eyes look on thee,
May they here extinguished be!
And then seven ravens
Pluck out the evil eyes;
Evil eyes (now) look on thee,
May they soon extinguished be!
Much dust in the eyes,
Thence may they become blind;
Evil eyes now look on thee,
May they soon extinguished be!
In the fire of God!

To find out if a child is suffering from the evil eye, hold the child as close as possible to the water in a running stream. Say:

Páñi, páñi sikova,
Dikh the upré, dikh, télé!
Buti páñi sikovel
Buti pál yákh the dikhel
Te ákáná mudárel.

Water, water, hasten!
Look up, look down!
Much water hastens
(May) as much come into the eye
Which looked evil on thee,
And may it now perish.

If the sound of the running water grows louder, the child is enchanted, but if the water sounds just as before, the difficulty lies elsewhere.

Charm to Cure a Toothache

Wind a barleystraw around a stone and throw it into a running brook while saying:

Oh dukh ándre m're dándá,
Tu ná báres cingerá!
Ná ává kiyá mánge,
Mire muy ná hin kere!
Tut ñikáná me kámáv,
Ač tu mánge pál páčá;
Káná e pçus yárpakri
Avel tele páñori!

Oh, pain in my teeth,
Trouble me not so greatly!
Do not come to me,
My mouth is not thy house.
I love thee not at all,
Stay away from me:
When this straw is in the brook
Go away into the water!

8

Gypsies and the Law

Gypsies have never been famous for observing the laws of the land—any land. They have been thieves, shoplifters, pickpockets, sellers of shoddy goods, swindlers of every sort—but hardly ever murderers or criminals of a very grievous sort. Their specialty has been petty crime, and, being quick, clever and deft, they are not too often caught. As a result they have been accused not only of the crimes they have committed, but of many others as well.

This may have come about because from the moment of their appearance in Europe. Gypsies were suspect, discriminated against, persecuted, treated as outcasts and pariahs. Or was it the other way around? *Were* Gypsies treated poorly because they were a strange minority group—or was it because they were thieves, shoplifters, pickpockets, et cetera? The case can be argued both ways, and we will never know the true answer.

As early as the fifteenth century a Bavarian writer named Adventin discussed Gypsies in this passage:

> . . . a race of men, a mixture of the scum of many nations, living by prey, whose home had originally been Turkey and Hungary and who are called Zigeuner, infested our countryside, living by thievery, robbery and magic.

As they traveled across Europe, the Gypsies established a pattern that was to be repeated over and over again. At first they were well received, because they carried with them impressive letters from heads of state or highly placed church officials urging that they be protected. But in a very short time the Gypsies wore out their welcome in all the countries they visited. They were driven out of cities to camp outside the walls. They were accused of vagrancy, robbery, heresy, beggary and even cannibalism. Strong repressive laws were passed against them, and by the mid-sixteenth century Gypsies were firmly established as outlaws.

In the Balkan countries matters were at their worst, for here, in the seventeenth century, Gypsies became slaves and were actually sold in slave markets. It was not until 1848 that this practice was outlawed in Roumania.

During this desperate time, terrified of becoming slaves, many Gypsies escaped the towns and hid in mountains and forests. They became even more secretive and furtive than they had been before. Whenever they did encounter gorgios, they communicated as little as possible, and if they were required to give information, they never gave it correctly. In this behavior Gypsies have never changed.

Bad as things were in the Balkans, and indeed in all countries, Gypsy persecution reached a climax under Adolf Hitler in modern Germany. When the Nazis began to intern Jews in concentration camps during the 1930s, they also rounded up Gypsies—and for some of the same "reasons." Hitler wanted to keep German blood "pure," to rid the country of its non-Aryan elements. As Hitler's armies raced across Europe, Gypsies were captured wherever they were found and brought back to the camps. At first they were subjected to "scientific" experiments and sterilized so that they could not have any children. Later, during World War II, they were exterminated in the gas ovens. It has been estimated that 400,000–600,000 Gypsies lost their lives at this time.

Hounded, chased, murdered, living outside the law for centuries—are Gypsies a totally lawless people? Not at all. They live in strict accordance with Gypsy law, the only law they recognize.

Borrow, in *The Zincali,* defines Gypsy law as follows:

Gypsy law divides itself into the three following heads or precepts:—

Separate not from *the husbands.*
Be faithful to *the husbands.*
Pay your debts to *the husbands.*

Borrow takes some of the mystery out of these ideas by explaining that the word *husbands* really means brethren. The first section of the law, then, he tells us, states that the Gypsy is to live with his own people and not with gorgios; he is to live in a tent as befits a wanderer, not in a house, which would tie him to one spot. He must in every respect conform to the ways of the Gypsies, and he must have nothing to do with gorgios except to tell them lies.

The second section, Borrow goes on to say, applies mostly to women. Romany women must be faithful to their men; otherwise the Romany race would soon disappear. Borrow points out that we can see well that this rule is observed just by looking at the British Gypsies. Although Romanies have been roving in England for three centuries, they are clearly different from the British in features and complexion.

The third section of the law, that dealing with debt, Borrow finds "highly curious." He says that the state of being in debt is called *pazorrhus* and it is something the Gypsies are very much ashamed of. He points out that ". . . a Gypsy will make the greatest sacrifices rather than remain pazorrhus to one of his brethren, even though he be of another clan."

Although written more than a century ago, Borrow's account of Gypsy law seems to be quite accurate. Among themselves, Gypsies are absolutely honorable.

Lacking written laws, law enforcement officers or courts, the Gypsy depends on tradition and the pressure of public (Gypsy) opinion to make his laws work. When a Gypsy has outraged his clan by a lawless act against another Gypsy, he may be excommunicated from the tribe. He is no longer permitted to travel with his group; he is not recognized if met or spoken to by any other Gypsy. Accompanied only by his wife and children, if any, he is doomed to travel alone forever. For a Gypsy, who fears loneliness more than anything else, this is truly a frightful punishment.

The state of excommunication is called *the shame* by English Gypsies, and it is certainly feared more than any prison term. Imprisoned by gorgios, the Gypsy still has the full respect of his tribe. Upon his release from jail he is treated like a martyr who has been made to suffer most unjustly. He is wined, dined, and nursed back to robust health and happiness. A Gypsy in the shame, however, has nothing to look forward to. As far as the tribe is concerned, he is not a Gypsy anymore and he can never become one again.

9

Some Gypsy Myths and Legends

The myths and legends of any people usually have a great deal to tell us about the people. With the Gypsies, however, we wind up, as always, with as many questions as answers. How old are Gypsy myths? Are they really ancient? Or are they relatively recent inventions with no basis at all in reality? If the latter, why have they remained alive?

One of the most often repeated Gypsy tales of all seems to spring from the New Testament. It concerns the nails that were used for the crucifixion of Christ, and it goes like this:

Yeshua ben Miriam (Jesus) was given over to the Roman jailers to be crucified because he had spoken disparagingly of the Roman emperor. Two soldiers were told to hurry out and get four strong nails, and they were given eighty kreutzers to pay a blacksmith to make the nails. But instead of going straight to the blacksmith, the soldiers went to the village tavern and spent half the money on wine. Then, in great haste and not overly sober, they rushed to get their errand done before nightfall.

When they came to a blacksmith's shop they called, "Hurry and make four big nails right away. We need them to crucify Yeshua ben Miriam."

Now the blacksmith was a Jew, and he didn't want Yeshua ben Miriam, another Jew, to be crucified, and so he said, "I cannot make the nails."

The soldiers were so angry that they set the Jew's beard on fire. Then they ran him through with their lances and hurried on their way.

When the soldiers came to a second blacksmith they said, "Make four strong nails for us. We will pay you forty kreutzer."

The blacksmith replied, "I cannot make strong nails for that price; I can only make small ones."

"Jew," the drunken soldiers shouted, "do as we say!" and they set his beard on fire.

Terrified, the smith reluctantly went to his forge to begin the work as one of the soldiers said, "Be sure to make the nails strong, because we have to crucify Yeshua ben Miriam in the morning."

But just at that moment the smith was able to hear the voice of the first blacksmith whom the soldiers had killed. It said, "Aria, do not make the nails. They are for one of our own people and he is innocent."

The Jew put down his hammer and said, "I cannot make nails to crucify Yeshua ben Miriam. I refuse."

Then the soldiers rushed upon the man and ran him through with their lances.

The third smith the soldiers came to was a Syrian. He had just begun to work on the nails when he heard the voices of the first two smiths. He put down his hammer, and soon he too was killed by the soldiers' lances.

Desperate, since it was nearly nightfall, the soldiers ran to the outskirts of Jerusalem. There, just beyond the gates, a Gypsy had pitched his tent for the night and set up an anvil. The soldiers put down the forty kreutzers and ordered the nails.

The Gypsy picked up the coins and put them in his pocket before he started to work. Then he finished three nails and had just started on the fourth when one of the soldiers said, "Thank you for making the nails. We will use them to crucify Yeshua ben Miriam."

At that moment the voices of the first three blacksmiths began to beg the Gypsy not to make the fourth nail. This time the soldiers heard the voices too, and were so frightened by the sound of the ghostly chorus that they ran off with the nails that were finished and didn't wait for the last one.

The Gypsy was glad he had pocketed the money first. He finished the fourth nail and waited for it to cool. To hurry it along he poured cold water over it, but the nail continued to glow as red as blood. He poured more and more water but nothing would cool the nail.

The Gypsy was frightened. Leaving the glowing nail on the ground, he took down his tent, packed it on his donkey and set out into the desert. Hours later he stopped by a well, and there at his feet he saw the glowing nail.

Now the Gypsy was crazy with fear. He fled farther and farther into the desert and finally pitched his tent near an Arab village. As soon as he set up his anvil, he saw the nail again. An Arab came with a broken wheel hoop for repair and the Gypsy fixed it with the glowing nail. Then he fled again until he came to Damascus. Months later, a man brought him a broken sword to repair, and the Gypsy mended it with the nail. Then he packed his tent and fled again.

For all time, the nail appears to the descendants of the man who forged the nails for the crucifixion of Yeshua ben Miriam—and they always flee. That is why Gypsies never stay in one place. And it is why Yeshua ben Miriam was crucified with only three nails instead of four. His tormentors had to use one nail to pierce both feet. The fourth nail still wanders the face of the earth just like the Gypsies.

There is another legend that deals with the crucifixion nail in quite a different way:

An old Gypsy woman watched the crucifixion procession as it passed by on its way to Calvary. She saw the suffering on Jesus's face and tried to free him by stealing the nails. She got the first one and threw it away, but when she tried to take the other three she was caught by the soldiers.

As she was being beaten, the old woman cried, "Please let me go. I haven't stolen anything for seven years."

Then one of the disciples said to the Gypsy, "The Saviour has blessed you. From now on, you are permitted to steal every seven years."

Jean-Paul Clébert, a French writer, suggests that Gypsy legends like these are pure fantasy and arise from the need of a rootless people to create ties. Since the Gypsies have forgotten their own past, they put their myths into biblical terms.

In another tale that follows this pattern, the Gypsies have cast themselves as Egyptians:

There was once a great Egyptian king called Pharaoh. He had many armies and used them to conquer country after country. But when he had conquered the whole world Pharaoh grew sad, because he loved war and there was no one left to war against.

Finally, Pharaoh thought that he would make war on God, so he dared Him to come down from Heaven with his angels to fight with Pharaoh and his armies.

God answered, "I will not measure my strength with that of a man." And God was angry and decided to punish Pharaoh. He made a large opening in the side of a mountain and then caused a violent windstorm. He forced Pharaoh and his soldiers into the hole, and the mountain closed over them. Whoever goes to that mountain on St. John's Night can still hear Pharaoh and his armies yelling inside the mountain.

And it came to pass that without Pharaoh's armies to keep them in bondage, all of the countries that had been conquered now rose up and conquered Egypt. They drove the Egyptians out of their land and sent them all over the world.

This myth offers an explanation of the original Gypsy dispersion from their native land, just as the first myth of the nails seeks to explain the nomadic life.

The following story covers both the dispersion and the wandering, and this time the native land is India.

When we lived on the Ganges, our chief had a son named Tchen.

The land of the Hind had a king whose favorite wife had given birth to a daughter named Gan. Now a sorcerer told the king that his land would be invaded by a man so strong that he would kill the king and conquer the country. The conqueror himself would be safe from all harm unless he harmed a Gypsy, in which case he would then die.

The king feared more for his infant daughter than for anyone else. To keep her safe he sent her to our chief, Tchen's father. The chief agreed to send the babe to the tent of the Gypsy chief, and no one but his wife would know who the little princess really was.

After a few days the chief of the Gypsies announced the birth of a daughter, Gan. She grew up in the same tent as Tchen.

When it was time for Tchen to choose a wife, all of the beautiful girls of the kingdom were brought before him. They performed their most intricate dances for him, but Tchen found none of the girls to his liking.

Then Tchen's father, the chief, died. It was important for Tchen to marry immediately, since the young chief must have a wife. But Tchen was in despair, for although there were many beautiful girls in the tribe, none was so beautiful as his sister.

At this time, Tchen's mother told him the truth, that Gan was not his sister after all, and so the pair were married. Since the truth was not told to anyone else, there was a great scandal in the land. Half the people vowed not to live under the rule of a chief who married his sister. The other half of the people were loyal to their king and said that no matter what he did it must be right. The people fought among themselves.

Now one of Skender's generals came like a wind into Hind, and just as the sorcerer had predicted, he killed the king and his wives and buried them all underneath the stones of their toppled palace.

Hearing of this man's brave exploits, one of the people of our own land went to see the conqueror to ask him what he thought of a chief who married his own sister. Enraged by the question, the general hit the man a great blow on the head.

As he did so, the general, together with the horse on which he sat, burst into the air and crumbled like dust on the ground.

Tchen and Gan were chased out of the land by those who were against them, but their followers all fled with them. These people became known as "Tchen-Gans." A great sorcerer cursed Tchen, Gan and all the Tchen-Gans. He decreed that they should forever wander the face of the earth, never sleep twice in the same place, never drink water twice from the same well and never twice cross the same river during any one year.

The following legend does not attempt to fill historical gaps, but instead explains the Gypsy profession of bear-leading. Exhibitors of trained bears are known as *ursari* in Romany and they are mentioned in the earliest reports of Gypsies.

Once upon a time, a young virgin became pregnant even though she had never had sexual relations with a man. Terrified, she went to drown herself in the river. But before she was able to throw herself into the water, a man sprang up from its depths. He told her not to be afraid, for she would give birth to an animal that could work like a man.

The girl went back to her camp, and later she gave birth to a bear. All of the members of the tribe helped her to teach it to dance and do tricks, and from that time on, the Gypsies were *ursari*.

This last legend, too, explains the beginning of a famed Gypsy profession, that of the violinist:

There was once a beautiful young girl who lived in the forest with her mother, her father and four brothers. Her name was Mara and she had the misfortune to fall in love with a gorgio who did not respond at all to her beauty or her love.

Beside herself, Mara decided to consult the devil. The devil agreed to help Mara on one condition—that she give up her family to the devil. Mara agreed.

The devil changed the four brothers into strings, the father into a sound box and the mother into a bow. The devil had indeed gained six souls, but he had also created the first violin. Mara soon learned to play the instrument, and her music was so divine that the gorgio was completely enchanted and fell madly in love with the lovely violinist.

But the devil was not content to see happiness. Untrue to his bargain, he reappeared and carried off the girl and her lover. The violin was left on the ground.

One day a poor Gypsy wandered by and saw the instrument. He picked it up and began to stroke it, and at once beautiful music poured forth. Having a profession at last, the Gypsy violinist traveled from village to village bringing tears and laughter to all who heard him.

10

Gypsies Today

Today, just as always, Gypsies maintain a life style that is uniquely their own. Whenever survival has demanded it, they have adapted—somewhat—to local conditions. In other words, they conform when they have to, but as little as possible.

In Czechoslovakia, a law passed in 1958 prohibits nomadism. Of an estimated 300,000 Czech Gypsies, about 56,000 still roam freely; many of the others are semi-sedentary. In Roumania the nomadic life is legal, but the law requires that all Gypsy children attend school. Here, many of the 100,000 to 200,000 Romanies stay in one place for at least some part of the school year.

Roumania has also passed a law that prohibits Gypsies from dealing in horses, the most traditional of all professions for Gypsies of this region. Now, many Roumanian Gypsies are dancers, musicians, coppersmiths, dealers in wool, knife-grinders, hod-carriers, factory hands, spoon-makers, merry-go-round owners. But regardless of laws and the adaptations, Gypsies are Gypsies. They are still as separate, still as mysterious as they were when they first appeared in Europe.

While there are never definite population figures for Gypsies, some recent estimates (from Bart McDowell) are: Bulgaria, 250,000; Hungary, 300,000; France, 100,000; Germany, 20-30,000; England, 15,000; and the United States of America, 50–100,000.

Considering that the Gypsy's inability to bear confinement has made him shun ships, it is somewhat surprising that so many braved the Atlantic crossing to reach the new world in the days before air travel. Actually, the first Gypsies to make the voyage had little choice in the matter, since they were deported from Europe during the seventeenth century, but large numbers came of their own free will to avoid persecution in eastern Europe during the nineteenth century.

The American Gypsy has adapted just like all the others. Instead of dealing in horses, which is hardly big business in America, the Gypsy is a used car dealer. And instead of fixing copper pots (how many Americans have copper pots?) he takes the dents out of auto fenders in one of the many Gypsy-owned auto body shops that abound in New York and other cities.

Some of the traditional professions have remained unaltered—fortune-telling, entertaining, peddling. Of the many Gypsies in large cities—New York, Los Angeles, Chicago, Boston, Portland and Toledo—a fair number are on welfare rolls; some engage in picking pockets or in some other form of petty thievery. And many seem to possess large amounts of wealth the source of which is another Romany mystery.

Some obviously well-to-do Gypsies recently entered a New York City jewelry store. There were children, parents, grandparents—about eight persons in all. The boys and men were dressed conventionally, and had they been alone, they probably would not have been noticed. The women, however, were stared at by everyone present. They wore American clothing which was *almost* ordinary if taken one item at a time. The overall effect was bizarre. They had on cloth winter coats with torn or motheaten fur collars. Their skirts were neither long nor short, not any fashionable length but just a "wrong" length, and they hung unevenly from below the coats. Their dresses or blouses were extremely low-cut in front, showing a slightly extraordinary amount of bosom, and they wore silk scarves around their heads and tied behind. But the most astonishing thing was the jewelry!

The Gypsy women were truly traveling banks, for there were twelve or fifteen diamond bracelets on each arm, huge diamond rings on every finger, ropes of diamonds, pearls, rubies and gold around each neck.

The grandmother wore an almost unbelievable watch.

It was about an inch and a half in diameter, with diamond numerals, a circlet of diamonds around the perimeter and a diamond bracelet about an inch wide. When a bystander admired the watch, the old woman flashed a gold-toothed smile and said, "You like it? Twenty-eight thousand." It was hard to tell whether she was offering it for sale or whether, in friendly fashion, she was boasting of the bargain she had bought.

After some fast and animated family conversation in Romany, the men of the group started negotiations for a $26,000 ring. The jeweler finally dropped the price to $16,000 and was obviously not prepared to sell for a penny less. The Gypsy men seemed resigned to that fact, but at this point the women took over the business and bargained strenuously for a further reduction of two dollars. They all seemed to be having a very good time.

According to one of the clerks in the shop, these same Gypsies come once or twice a year to make large purchases, and the jeweler always raises the prices to begin with so that the bargaining can be carried on in satisfactory style. The clerk also said that the family travels the country in a fleet of Cadillacs, sleeping at campsites or in the cars. He said too that no matter how many jewels they bought, they always paid for them in cash.

When questioned directly about the family's travels, the mother of the children stated that they never travel at all but live in a house in New Jersey. The younger boy later remarked that he had been born in Paris.

Gypsies do not leave each other in time of trouble. If one of their tribe is ill, the clan gathers at the hospital and does not leave. When visiting hours are over they wait in the lobby, men, women and children, sleeping on chairs, benches and bare marble floors. They keep up the vigil for weeks at a time if necessary. And they pay all bills, no matter how large, in cash.

This article by Bernard Weinraub which appeared in the *New York Times* on April 13, 1971, makes an appropriate closing word for this book. It shows us clearly that after half a millennium the Gypsy is what he always was—separate, apart, the dark and mysterious stranger.

EUROPE'S LONG-HARASSED GYPSIES, ENDING PARLEY, SEEK WORLD RECOGNITION OF 'SEPARATE WAY OF LIFE'

LONDON, April 12—Gypsies, plagued for years by hostile laws and harassment, are pressing for international recognition and a new consciousness of their plight across Europe.

At the conclusion today of the first international congress of gypsies since 1935, gypsy leaders from 15 countries vowed to prepare reports for the United Nations Commission on Human Rights as well as the Council of Europe—an 18-nation intergovernmental group that seeks to promote European unity—and to press European governments for some form of recognition.

"The danger to gypsies is no longer bombs or bayonets but the assimilation policies of European governments," said Gratton Puxon, 31-year-old secretary of the British Gypsy Council. "What is needed is international recognition that gypsies are a separate people with a separate way of life."

The gypsy conference, held in Orpington, Kent, outside of London, ended when representatives of the three million European Romanies, or gypsies, traveled to Hampstead Heath in northern London for a music festival and a gypsy marriage.

EMPHASIS ON THE FUTURE

"We paid tribute at our conference to the 500,000 gypsies who died in German concentration camps," Vanko Rouda, president of the International Gypsy Committee, said on the outdoor site as bearded men began playing balalaikas and barefoot girls with rings on each finger began dancing.

"But we also look forward to the future, to the new consciousness of our young," he said. "The marriage of two young gypsy people symbolizes the future of our race."

The harassment of gypsies—who are either dark-skinned Romanies descended from a wandering Indian tribe or Irish "tinkers" who turned nomadic after last century's potato famine in Ireland—was the central issue at the World Romany Congress.

'IT'S MY WHOLE LIFE'

In discussing the "awakening nationalism" of gypsies across Europe, the delegates pressed for a standardized Romany language to be taught at schools on caravan sites, the establishment of an international gypsy newspaper, and efforts to avoid yielding to the alien way of life of what they term gorgios, or house dwellers.

"Gypsies must control their own destinies," said Mr. Puxon, a key figure in the international gypsy movement. He is the son of a Suffolk lawyer and is a gypsy by choice, not birth.

"It just happens that my view of life is very much like that of gypsies," he said. "I look at society now and I see progressive people wanting to escape from conformity. I'm against the centralization of government; the bureaucracy is too consolidated. I couldn't possibly do anything else now. It's my whole life.

"In eastern Europe there are laws against nomads, except in Yugoslavia," said Mr. Puxon. "They've tried to settle gypsies and prevent people from traveling."

After the conference, the gypsy leaders said that the main problem for gypsies in western Europe had been scarcity of legal camping sites.

In Britain, for example, with 20,000 gypsies, Mr. Puxon and others are pressing for 200 permanent sites instead of the present 40, and are hoping to build nursery schools and caravan schools for the 6,000 gypsy children in Britain and Wales.

Fewer than 600 children now attend school and many are growing up illiterate.

A Glossary of English Romany

adray	there
akai	here
ake	there is
alev	name
ande	into
andre	inside
ari	gold
arva	yes
atch	to stop, to make camp
atching-tan	camping place
atoot	across
atrashed	afraid
auko	here
avree	away, outside

baula-moosh	pig keeper
baula-moosh-engro	pork butcher
bavol	the wind
bender	tent, sticks for a tent
beren	ship
beren-engro	sailor
besh	to sit
bibi	aunt
bichadey-pawdel	banishment, prison
bicken	to sell
bister	a summons
bisterin' moosh	magistrate
bok	luck
bokky	lucky
boler	wheel
boobi	pea
bor	friend
boro	big, high
boro divvas	great day (holiday, wedding day, etc.)
boro doriav	ocean
boro-drom	highway
boro-gavaste	city (big town)
boro-rani	big lady
boro-rye	big man (Sir, Lord)
bosh	violin
boshomengro	violinist
bouri	hedge
bouri-cannie	pheasant (hedge chicken)

bouri-pennen	conference (gathering under the hedge)
bun	witch
busni	non-Gypsies
cannie	chicken
chai	woman
chal	boy
chavi	child
chi	girl
chib	language
chin	to cut
chiv	knife
choovahani	witch
chop	to swap, trade, exchange
chor	to steal
coor	to fight
covantza	anvil
dadrus	father
dai	mother
dav	to give
del	to hit
didakai	half-breed Gypsy
dik	look, see
dikker-glim	looking glass
diklo	handkerchief, neckerchief
dinelo	silly
divio	crazy
divvus	day
dloova	money

doriav	sea
drahengro	doctor (poison-maker)
drom	road
dui	two
duk	hand
dukkerin	fortune-telling
Duvel	God
engro	maker
fakir	worker, mender
gad	shirt
gavaste	town
gaver	policeman
gillie	song
giv	farm
givengro	farmer
gorgio	non-Gypsy
groi	horse
groi-engro	horse-dealer
gyas	she
haw	to eat
hotchi-witchi	hedgehog
jaul	go, travel
jaul the drom	travel the road
jib	speech, language
jin	to know, understand
jivaben	life
jukal	dog
juval	woman
kairengro	house-dweller

kako	uncle
kash	wood
kash yag	wood fire
kauli (kali)	dark, black
kavvi	kettle
kavvi saster	kettle iron
kek	no
kekeno moosh	nobody
kenner	house
kennik	house-dweller
kep	bed
kil	to play
kitchema	inn
kooshti	good
kooshti Duvel	the good God
kosh	stick
kova	thing
kushti	good
kuster	to ride
lav	word
lekki	his or her
lel	to take
levinkor	beer
lil	book
lir	cheap
loli	red
lon	salt
lulagis	flowers
mandi	me

mastengro	butcher
matchki	fish
matchko	cat
maung	to beg
merno	mine
moosh	man
mullah	ghost
mulled	dead
mulled-moosh-engro	doctor (dead man maker)
mullerdi puv	cemetery (field of the dead)
mumper	tramp
nafli	ill
nanti	never
nav	name
noki	either
ochemengri	frying pan
odi	all
opre	up
panni	water
panni gurni	frog
patteran (patrin)	leaf
peeve	to drink
pen	to speak, say
pen	sister
pennen	telling
petulengro	blacksmith
phral	brother
pirri	foot
plastramengro	policeman

plen	hill
pobbo	apple
poci	pocket
pogado	broken
pogado jib	Romany-English
pooker	speech, talk
pooro	old
posh	half
posh-rat	half-breed Gypsy (literally half-blood)
praster	to run
puv	field, ground
puvengra	potato
rackli	girl
racklo	woman
rani	lady
rat	blood
rati	night
rikkeni	beautiful
rocker	to speak, talk
rom	husband, male
Romanes	Romany language
Romani	Gypsy
Romanichai	Gypsy woman
Romanichal	Gypsy man
rommer	to marry
rommerin	wedding
rovel	wife
ruckers	trees

ruckersamengri	squirrel (tree creature)
san	are
sapengro	snake-charmer
sar shan?	how do you do?
sasto	well
sastra	iron
sherengro	chief
shooshie	rabbit
solivardo	light cart
sor	elderly
svegla	pipe
taddivas	today
tan	tent
tarni	young
tarno	little
tarots	fortune-telling cards
tasaulor	tomorrow
tatcho	true, real
tatchipen	truth
tele	down
toot, tooti	you
toovla	tobacco
trin	three
truppo	body
vardo	living-wagon, caravan
vek	with
veshengro	gamekeeper
wafodi	bad
wast	hand

welgora	horse fair
wonger	money, coal
woodrus	bed
wooster	throw
yag	fire
yanaheim	lucky words
yock	eye
yogengri	gun
yorya	egg

Bibliography

Bercovici, Konrad, *The Story of the Gypsies.* London: Jonathan Cape, 1929.

Block, Martin, *Gypsies, Their Life and Their Customs.* (Trans. by Kuczynski and Taylor.) New York and London: D. Appleton-Century, 1939.

Borrow, George, *The Romany Rye.* London: The Cresset Press, 1948.

Borrow, George, *The Zincali, An Account of the Gypsies of Spain.* New York: Scribner and Welford, 1888.

Clébert, Jean-Paul, *The Gypsies.* Baltimore: Penguin 1967. (Trans. by Charles Duff from *Les Tsiganes.* Paris: Arthaud, 1961.)

Leland, Charles Godfrey, *Gypsy Sorcery and Fortune-Telling.* London: Unwin, 1891. Reprint: New York: Dover, 1971.

McDowell, Bart. *Gypsies, Wanderers of the World.* Washington, D. C.: National Geographic Society, 1970.

Petulengro, Gypsy, *A Romany Life.* New York: Dutton, 1936.

Serboianu, C. J. Popp, *Les Tsiganes.* Paris: Payot, 1930.

Starkie, Walter, *Raggle Taggle.* New York: Dutton, 1933.

Webb, G. E. C., *Gypsies, the Secret People.* London: Herbert Jenkins, 1960.

Yoors, Jan, *Gypsies.* New York: Simon & Schuster, 1967.

Index

About the Author

BERNICE KOHN was born in Philadelphia and attended the University of Wisconsin. She is the author of more than thirty books for young people and for a time was an editor of children's science books. Among some of her recent titles are THE BEACHCOMBER'S BOOK, THE AMISTAD MUTINY, HOW HIGH IS UP? and OUT OF THE CAULDRON: A SHORT HISTORY OF WITCHCRAFT.

Miss Kohn is the mother of three children, all of whom are fascinated by Gypsy lore. She lives in Manhattan and East Hampton with her husband, Morton Hunt, an author of adult books.